Negotiating Culture in Organizational Change

Tamaro Green

Contents

This research reviews emerging research in cultural psychology and cross-cultural management studies to recommend negotiation of culture in organizational change. Organizations may partner with public institutions or other organizations and negotiation of this partnership with cultural awareness may improve communication and creativity. The research begins with a brief introduction to the fields of cultural psychology and cross-cultural management. The research continues to provide a review of research in organizational change. The research then proposes a model for negotiating culture in organizational change. The research provides a risk assessment for testing and evaluating the model and concludes with recommendations for negotiation of culture in organizational change.

Introduction

Negotiation of culture in organizational change may implement cultural psychology and cross-cultural management studies to improve communication and strategy for organizations (Gelfand, Aycan, Erez, & Leung, 2017). Ciuculescu and LUCA (2022) describe how municipal officials can implement cultural strategies for location branding capable of improving tourism and industry. Gelfand et al. (2017) review the history of research in cultural psychology for industries and organizations. Huang (2010) explain the importance of awareness of potential problems in business communication across cultures.

Measurement of cultural influence may be a challenge for traditional psychological approaches (Smith & Bond, 2022). Fatehi, Priestley, and Taasoobshirazi (2020) validate constructs for measurements of differences in cultural communication as horizontal and vertical, individualism and collectivism. Smith and Bond (2022) discuss the limitations of measuring culture in social psychology research. Berry (2022) proposes psychological human behavior should be measured in a view of contexts which include community, family, and individual levels. Dasen (2022) describes a trend in psychology towards physical sciences and less approaches to studies across cultures.

The inclusion of culture in management research may improve communication and opportunities for organizational change (Altarriba & Basnight-Brown, 2022). Barmeyer, Bausch, and Moncayo (2019) observe the growth of cross-cultural management from fields of research such as international management and comparative management. Somerville, Cinite, and Largacha-Martínez (2021) compare individualistic and collective cultures in their ability to embrace organizational change. Altarriba and Basnight-Brown (2022) emphasizes the importance of language in communication across cultures.

Review of Emerging Research

Emerging research in fields of sociology, psychology and management support strategies for negotiating culture in organizational change (Essawi & Tilchin, 2012; Prieto-Díeza, Postigoa, Cuestaa, & Muñiz, 2022). Essawi and Tilchin (2012) develop a collaborative model for implementing organizational change. Prieto-Díeza et al. (2022) discuss personality traits as a measure of work engagement. Lafaire, Kuismin, Moisander, and Grünbaum (2022) propose techniques of artistic intervention to encourage engagement in education. Mousseau (2021) suggests globalization and legislation may reduce ethnic conflicts by reducing power of national states.

Organizational culture may be viewed as the norms of the organization (Taylor, Suminski, Das, Paxton, & Craig, 2018). Taylor et al. (2018) distinguish levels of beliefs, values, assumptions, and norms which compromise an organizational culture. Tsai (2011) empirically explore relationships between qualitative measures of job satisfaction and leadership styles. Hall, Brazil, Wakefield, Lerer, and Tennen (2010) confirm opposing relationships between high turnover rates and job satisfaction in a study of organizational culture. Maseko (2017) evaluate the extents of organizational culture.

Negotiating culture may also be viewed a promotion of workplace health (Taylor et al., 2018). Taylor et al. (2018) describe workplace health promotion as a part of organizational culture. Pedrosa et al. (2020) evaluate the emotional, behavioral, and psychological effects of the health pandemic. Resnik and Elliott (2016) suggest the importance of researchers to recognize and exercise social responsibility in scientific fields. Inegbedion, Sunday, Asaleye, Lawal, and Adebanji (2020) propose a model for diversity management in organizational efficiency. Green and Seher (2003) observe

limitations in the literature of research areas in ethnic

violence and social psychology of prejudice.

Negotiating culture in organization may require

strategies for resolving conflicts in workplace to serve

employees and stakeholders (Momanyi & Juma, 2016;

Wang & Wu, 2020). Momanyi and Juma (2016) identify

different styles of conflicts in workplace environments.

Colvin (2011) empirically evaluates the outcomes of

employment arbitration. Wang and Wu (2020) explore

internal conflict within an organization to promote conflict

management proposals based on the stakeholders of an

organization. Siebert and Herbst (2021) recommend

techniques for identifying additional issues in negotiation

with a weighted mathematical approach.

Studies may improve international mediation and

provide strategies for negotiating culture in organizational

change (Alexander & Tunkel, 2022; Popoola & Karadas,

2022). Popoola and Karadas (2022) research how perceptions of societal limitations can influence notions of career success. Alexander and Tunkel (2022) discuss how legal and cultural differences can affect international contract mediation. Quirico (2021) describe how regional organizations may play a role in international trade agreements between countries.

Negotiating culture for organizations may pursue acceptance of limitations in implementing organizational change (Edwards & Saltman, 2017). Edwards and Saltman (2017) discusses some of the challenges in organizational change in public institutions. Edwards and Saltman (2017) review conflicts for political decision makers in public institutions for resources, budget limitations, sustainability, and customer service. Chea (2006) promotes strategies for identifying positive benefits in organizational conflicts such as to create innovative ideas, promote organizational change, and develop effective managers. Patton (2018) differentiates between destructive and constructive conflict. Patton (2018) discusses organizational design to solve imbalances of strategies, structure, processes, people, and rewards within an organization. Vähä-Savo, Luomanen, and Alasuutari (2022) explore rationalism and romanticism in the logic of organizational conflict.

Research in cultural empathy may improve organizational change within enterprises (Delpechitre, 2013). Delpechitre (2013) explores cultural empathy and cultural assimilation. Brunelle (2013) draws relationships between physical distance and psychological influence in environments of supervisors and subordinates. Arrojo (2021) highlights attributes of enterprise social knowledge systems.

Negotiating culture in organizational change may value from institution through education (Babalis & Lazarakou, 2021). Oguejiofor (2012) discuss a philosophic dialogue that existed between ancient African and Greek cultures. Mabovula Nonceba (2011) reviews awareness of the theoretical framework of the African philosophy of Ubuntu and communalism. Babalis and Lazarakou (2021) define historical empathy as a tool for the education of controversial topics in history. Mudave (2016) compare educational institution information literacy programs around the world.

Issues of ethics and multicultural necessities may be integrated early in information technology design to improve outcomes (Israel & Amer, 2021). Israel and Amer (2021) describe the failure of adaptations to existing technological infrastructures for multicultural needs in comparison to the potential success of building multicultural systems from inception. Israel and Amer (2021) discussed an approach of digital hermeneutics to explore and evaluate ethics in information technology culture. Ethical issues may require advanced design with emerging technologies (Nyholm, 2018). Nyholm (2018) explores some of the ethical dilemmas that may arise with autonomous vehicles. The health pandemic has also introduced new dilemmas for technology design (Chan, 2021). Chan (2021) explores knowledge management tools as techniques for responding to the business, social, and technology impacts of the health pandemic.

Institutions of higher education may heed recommendations for inclusive and lifelong curricula design (Cronholm, 2021; Karp Gershon, Ruipérez-Valiente, & Alexandron, 2021). Cronholm (2021) recommends higher education institutions design programs for promoting lifelong learning. Karp Gershon et al. (2021) supports inclusive design processes for massively open online course curricula.

Techniques for improving curricula design may also include promotion, openness, and assessment (Della-Piana, Gardner, & Mayne, 2018; Laakso & Polonioli, 2018; Negoita, Rahrovani, Lapointe, & Pinsonneault, 2021).

Negoita et al. (2021) describe increased efforts in promoting information technology implementation in project planning as a strategy for information technology projects. Laakso and Polonioli (2018) evaluate the open access policies of journals in ethics research to measure open access availability. Della-Piana et al. (2018) identify techniques for connecting classroom and large-scale assessments such as including complex tasks, automated scoring, and improved reporting.

Model for Negotiation of Culture

Negotiation of culture in organizational change may be reviewed as a field for allowing the development or renewal of an organizational culture (Harikkala-Laihinen, 2022). Harikkala-Laihinen (2022) evaluates the effectiveness of programs and their coordination through the viewpoint of the client as a recipient of change. Bos-de Vos, Deken, and Kleinsmann (2022) evaluate roles and procedures for organizational system transformation programs. Shah, Shah, and El-Gohary (2022) evaluate organizational learning and innovation for small and medium sized businesses. Korenkiewicz and Maennig (2022) provide an empirical study of customer satisfaction indices to determine effects of executive level gender diversity.

Strategies for evaluating corporate performance many include measuring innovation, supply chains, and corporate social responsibility (Friesenbichler & Hoelzl, 2022; Maury, 2022; Zhang & Xie, 2022). Cultural negotiation may be included as a measure of corporate social responsibility. Zhang and Xie (2022) measure the influence of environmentally sustainable practices on supply chains. Maury (2022) explores the benefits of strategies for firms to practice corporate social responsibility. Friesenbichler and Hoelzl (2022) reviews influences to the growth of firms such as innovation and efficiency.

Research evaluates emerging roles for improving corporate social responsibility (Urquhart, 2019; Zhang, 2022). Urquhart (2019) provides suggestions for improving corporate image for the tourism industry. Zhang (2022) measures the effects of corporate social responsibility on corporate image and customer loyalty and satisfaction. Dawood, Liew, and Lau (2021) provide a systemic literature review of for studies of measuring trust and doubt of customers in relationship to corporate social responsibility. Sousa, Marôco, Gonçalves, and Machado (2022) evaluate the potential for digital learning to be part of sustainable education.

Negotiation of culture in organizational change may improve the ability for firms to adapt with effective models (Kuehnel & Au-Yong-Oliveira, 2022; McKenzie, 2022). Kuehnel and Au-Yong-Oliveira (2022) suggest agile models for organizational structure for companies to adapt to consumer, manufacturing, and environmental demands more easily. Lv, Liu, and Xu (2019) demonstrate technology and globalization lead to lower growth in inflation. McKenzie (2022) proposes methods for evaluating influence in the entertainment industry.

Sugianto and Pontjoharyo (2020) describe how lean processes can support organizational cultural change. Kwet (2020) propose government policies to transform a democratic commons ecosystem from social media platforms. Fink, Shao, Lichtenstein, and Haefliger (2020) describe the advantage of software libraries for innovation by providing tools for experimentation and prototyping. Jaramillo, Rascon, Adams, and Jauregui (2020) develop a software testing strategy that is capable of qualifying applications in complex technology environments.

Models for negotiating culture in organizational change may reflect measures of circularity and sustainability (Babri, Corvellec, & Stål, 2022). Babri et al. (2022) draw relationships between measures of circularity and sustainability in business models. Allcott, Gentzkow, and Yu (2019) produce an empirical analysis of the spread of misinformation in political process. Franco and Pound (2022) review social dominance theory in evaluation of group-based social hierarchies. Manstead (2018) describe conflicts which may arise from socioeconomic class structures in universities. Madva (2016) suggests promoting interaction among class structures to reduce individualism.

Understanding and mitigating bias may be essential for effective development of the model for negotiating culture in organizational change. Pager and Shepherd (2008) explore potential measures for empirical analyses of discrimination. Abd-Elrhaman and Ghoneimy (2018) list conflict management and communication skills essential to effective patient care in healthcare organizations. FitzGerald and Hurst (2017) explain a prevalence of implicit biases in healthcare professionals and the ability for biases and stereotypes to affect judgement and behavior. Blair et al. (2021) provide an experimental study on the effect of religious messages to influence personal attitudes and intended behaviors. Baltaci (2017) describe cultural intelligence as the ability to achieve in a variety of cultural and multi-cultural settings. Alrababa'H, Marble, Mousa, and Siegel (2021) assess the influence of exposure to celebrity figures for improving awareness of diverse cultures and reducing prejudice.

The model for negotiating culture in organizational change may be reviewed as conflict resolution strategy. Whitehorn (2020) review a conflict management checklist which consists of defining the conflict, identifying organizational and personal factors, self-reflection, clarification, and communication. Keet and Grütter (2021) evaluate the possibility of recycling ontologies in conflict resolution frameworks. Ji (2022) measures effectiveness of blended learning models. Harris, Pattillo, and Sykes (2022) discover monetary sanctions preserve and aggravate inequalities. Angelos, Devon, Ferreres, McLeod, and Ellison (2021) describe trust as key to ethical decision making in academic leadership.

Studies in conflict resolution management may include research in diplomacy. Hoshiro (2020) study the influence of diplomatic relations on the allocation of international foreign aid. Ličen and Slapničar (2022) study process accountability as a strategy for mitigating risk in decision making. Opie and Roberts (2017) develop a restorative justice framework towards repairing harm and rebuilding trust in organizations and institutions.

Negotiation of culture in organizational change may also be viewed as a strategy involving diplomacy. Hoshiro (2020) study the influence of diplomatic relations on the allocation of international foreign aid. Ličen and Slapničar (2022) study process accountability as a strategy for mitigating risk in decision making. Opie and Roberts (2017) develop a restorative justice framework towards repairing harm and rebuilding trust in organizations and institutions.

Negotiating culture in organizational change may create more responsibilities for the boards which review academic research. Page and Nyeboer (2017) review the roles of research ethics boards which may consist of institutional review boards or research ethics committees. Ralefala, Ali, and Kass (2018) studied the views of researchers on institutional review boards and highlight advantages in the process for appreciating research ethics and ethical review processes. Kästner et al. (2015) recommend a more standardized approach to the institutional review board process for vulnerable populations to coincide workflows and decision times. Mhaskar, B Bercu, and Djulbegovic (2013) examine the level of expertise for institutional review board members for randomized control trials. Park et al. (2018) present implementing quality assurance in to manage good clinical practice in medical research. Suelzer, Deal, Hanus, Ruggeri, and Witkowski (2021) review retracted articles in medical journals for publishing ethics. Feldman (2014) discuss challenges for institutional review boards in social and behavioral sciences as they were designed for medical research. Gordon (2020) presents categorical and contextual approaches for institutional review boards to

protect rights of participants in studies. Nerlinger et al.

(2018) propose an advocacy portfolio for physicians to

demonstrate the impact of their scholarly projects on health

outcomes.

Evaluations and Assessment of Risk

Negotiation of culture in organizational change may mitigate risks presented if organizations present a negative environment for inclusion. Zheng and Chun (2017) study repeated patterns of corporate misconduct and highlight how corporate misconduct negatively impacts other organizations and society. Orlitzky, Louche, Gond, and Chapple (2015) measure corporate social performance based on a number of stakeholders including customers, communities, shareholders, suppliers, environmentalists, and employees. Paolella and Durand (2016) measure how well corporations are able to perform spanning over a number of categories versus focus on one specialty area.

Ethics in management may be a formidable component of improving organizational through corporate governance (Puiu & Ogarca, 2015). Puiu and Ogarca (2015) describe a lack of implementation of ethics management to be a component leading to corruption. Herrington and Coduras (2019) describe corruption as a component inhibiting entrepreneurial opportunities for small businesses. Oye (2013) discusses ways that information communication technologies can curtail corruption in government such as by publicizing information, providing monitoring, and sharing data.

Negotiation of culture in organizational change may combat corruption by reducing nepotism, preventing abuse, increasing productivity, and increasing justice (Omar Bali, 2018). Subramanyam and Dasaraju (2014) suggest detailed disclosure requirements to improve transparency in corporate governance. Ceresia and Mendola (2019) explain how perceptions of a lack of enforcement of corrupt activities can impact entrepreneurial activity.

Negotiation of culture in organizational change may limit corruption in public institutions (Liu, 2016). Liu

(2016) discusses measures that can reduce corruption such as decentralizing organizations, increasing competition, providing information, extending terms of local officials, and increasing public sector salaries. Boles (2014) provides examples of corruption as fraud, money laundering, illegal cartels, misstating financial statements, bribery, and exacting undue influence. Bouchard, Kohler, Orbinski, and Howard (2012) explain that corruption in health care may reduce access to adequate health services.

Gender representation and pay gaps may improve strategies for negotiation of organizational culture (World Economic Forum, 2016). World Economic Forum (2016) reports that women represent 5% of CEOs and 19% of board members in the information and communication technology sector while representing 24% of the workforce in the sector. Erosa, Fuster, and Restuccia (2016) mention that the gender gap in wages increases in age with wage increases for men at a rate of 2.1 and women at a rate of 1.7

over a 20 year period. Erosa et al. (2016) also find that men work more hours in a week, at an average of 37.6 versus 26.7 for women. Quffa (2016) identified that a 2013 study found that women working full-time were paid 78% of what men were paid.

Negotiation of organizational culture may promote more effective measures and regulations for reducing deficiencies in pay differences (Gürerk, Irlenbusch, & Rockenbach, 2018). Gürerk et al. (2018) explain that when business teams have a majority of women, studies have shown, they tended to be more generous, cooperative, responsive to experimental conditions, and invested in social sustainability initiatives Gürerk et al. (2018) identified in their experimental study that men tend to be more motivated by greed and women tend to be more motivated by fear. Quffa (2016) mentions that the Lilly Ledbetter Fair Pay Act of 2009, an amendment to the Civil

Rights Act of 1964, allows employers to be liable for discrimination in employment.

Data analysis and risk assessment may support negotiation of culture in organizational change decision processes (Mayowa, 2020). Mayowa (2020) discuss the benefits of data sources for informed management decisions. Organizations that have data available to make informed decisions can also integrate data into their risk assessment models. Models for risk assessment can also include organization behavioral models. One example of this model, is a model for bargaining behavior (Sawa, 2020). Sawa (2020) explore utility and prospect theories in developing a model for bargaining behavior.

Negotiation of culture in organization may integrate risk assessment into their innovation strategies. The risk assessment can be broad enough to include partnerships with other organizations as these strategic partnerships are often instrumental to the success of an organization.

Alexandre Royer (2020) followed the leadership success of one organization and found the ability to develop partnerships to share the workload of innovation to be one of the advantageous components. Partnerships may be evaluated for international and organizational effectiveness (Leal Filho et al., 2022). Leal Filho et al. (2022) evaluate the potential for international partnerships in achieving goals for regional organizations.

Human resource management may also benefit from research on organizational culture risk assessments (Boon, Den Hartog, & Lepak, 2019). Boon et al. (2019) review the literature of human resource management systems and develop frameworks to identify areas that may require further research. Human resource management systems may include tools for supporting the organization in crisis situations. Further research in human resource management and crisis management may improve organizational risk management (Boon et al., 2019; Bundy,

Pfarrer, Short, & Coombs, 2016). Bundy et al. (2016) explain limitations in research in large scale crisis management.

Human resource management may be a critical component for developing negotiation of culture teams. Haslinda (2009) explores the development of the terms human resource management and human resource development.Rohilla (2017) describes advantages for information technology in human resource management for planning, recruitment, training, and operations. Randall, Lartey, and Tate (2020) compare generation gaps in the psychological benefits of enterprise social media platforms. Ma and Cheng (2020) evaluate the success of implementing psychological contracts between employers and employees.

Public relations may also be a critical factor for organizational culture risk assessment models (Morehouse, 2020). Morehouse (2020) explores crisis communication and public relations in organizational crisis management.

A crisis communication strategy may benefit the organization internally and the relationship of the organization with the community.

Financial risk management may be included in an organizational change risk assessment model (Coulmont, Berthelot, & Talbot, 2020). Coulmont et al. (2020) described the growth of countries requiring financial risk disclosures in the annual reports of companies. Organizational financial risk management may also be integrated with financial institutional risk management systems. The finance risk of institutions by banks may present a model for organizational financial risk management models. For example, banks may provide different models for managing financial risk. Erülgen, Rjoub, and Adalıer (2020) compared how large and small banks utilize foreign investments, interest income, and liquid assets.

Conclusion and Recommendations

A number of approaches can support negotiating culture in organizational change such as studies in language, indigenous groups, and leadership styles (Boca, Radulescu, Toader, & Toader, 2015; Chiu, 2017; Lewin, 2014). Developing and evaluating organizational models with risk managements may improve the efficiency of negotiating culture. Chiu (2017) suggests the importance of including indigenous studies in cross-cultural management research. Boca et al. (2015) suggest flexible leadership to promote cultural sensitivity, effective communication, and creativity within organizations. Lewin (2014) describes how differences in management practices can vary due to national structures. Gerhart (2009) suggests differences among nations of the effects of national culture on organizational culture may be minimal. Huang, de Vliert, and der Vegt (2005) compare across nations the interest of employees to mention important issues for an organization. Romani, Mahadevan, and Primecz (2018) propose consolidating cross-cultural management studies into a field capable of reflecting alternate perceptions of culture.

Negotation of culture in organizational change may include resolving gender pay gap in information technology may be creating more post graduate opportunities for women, creating more opportunities that do not rely on programming skills, and making changes to curriculum in academic institutions (Glover & Guerrier, 2010; Mittal, 2016; Naranjo-Cantabrana, Ayala-Bobadilla, & Castro-Borunda, 2014). Glover and Guerrier (2010) highlights that when information technology was in its infancy, women had a higher representation than today. Glover and Guerrier (2010) explain that as the demand for programmers in information technology grew, the representation for women in the field became lower. Mittal (2016) explore mobile technologies in encouraging women to learn about climate smart technologies to make decisions about climate change in agriculture. Naranjo-Cantabrana et al. (2014) recorded in a study of an academic institution that men felt they had better opportunities for post graduate studies. Dowd (2000) suggests that uniform college grading in quantitative and non-quantitative fields may be a potential strategy for reducing the gender pay gap.

Negotiation of culture in organizational change may also be integrated in digital transformations (Crandall, North, & Crandall, 2020). Crandall et al. (2020) discover that data collection is one of the highest ranked challenges for school counselors in the digital transformation of education. Iivari, Sharma, and Ventä-Olkkonen (2020) explain how the digital divide has created a challenge for basic education during the pandemic. Mirbabaie, Bunker, Stieglitz, Marx, and Ehnis (2020) examine how social media is perceived during a time of crisis. Córdoba-Pachón

(2020) describes how systems thinking design can be influenced by strategies developed during the pandemic.

Research in organizational change may be valuable for identifying strategies for implementing cultural awareness. Hamdani (2021) review components such as environment, training, and competence to influence entrepreneurial motivation. Shah, Amjed, and Jaboob (2020) evaluate the role of entrepreneurial education in encouraging characteristics for entrepreneurship. Addo (2022) discuss challenges in depending on technological ecosystems to address societal issues.

Negotiating cultural differences through partnerships with public and private, national, regional and international organizations may also support successful organizational change strategies. Emerging research evaluates partnerships between public institutions and private companies (van Gestel, Oomens, & Buwalda, 2019). van Gestel et al. (2019) describe the growth of public-private partnerships for labor markets. Roy (2021) discusses challenges of contemporary political systems such as biased citizen perspectives, political disengagement, and participatory inequality. Woodhouse, Belardinelli, and Bertelli (2022) evaluate the effectiveness of public-private partnerships in delivering public services.

Research in partnerships between public institutions and private partnerships may include effects on civic participation. Concilio, Costa, Karimi, Vitaller del Olmo, and Kehagia (2022) describe international limitations of access to public services for immigrants, refugees, and asylum seekers. Robison (2022) assess components for the development of personal civic duties. Tagaki (2017) employ action research to draft policies to improve civic participation of people with disabilities with meetings. George, Walker, and Monster (2019) evaluate research in strategic planning for organizational performance.

Negotiating culture in organizational change may face challenges within public organizations (Edwards & Saltman, 2017). Edwards and Saltman (2017) discusses some of the challenges in organizational change in public institutions. Edwards and Saltman (2017) review conflicts for political decision makers in public institutions for resources, budget limitations, sustainability, and customer service. Chea (2006) promotes strategies for identifying positive benefits in organizational conflicts such as to create innovative ideas, promote organizational change, and develop effective managers. Patton (2018) differentiates between destructive and constructive conflict. Patton (2018) discusses organizational design to solve imbalances of strategies, structure, processes, people, and rewards within an organization. Vähä-Savo et al. (2022) explore rationalism and romanticism in the logic of organizational conflict.

Negotiating culture through organizational change may rely on improving management practices (de la Cuesta-González, Froud, & Tischer, 2020). de la Cuesta-González et al. (2020) develop a theoretical framework for identifying how public action can influence behaviors by corporations. Kimseng, Javed, Jeenanunta, and Kohda (2020) provide an empirical study of qualitative data for a comparative analysis of human resource management practices.

Negotiating culture through processes such as organizational change, corporate social responsibility, and entrepreneurship may benefit from studies in ethics and philosophy (Coeckelbergh, 2021; Mühlhoff, 2021). Mühlhoff (2021) explores how predictive analytics can be developed in a manner that does not enforce discriminatory behaviors. Coeckelbergh (2021) explores the philosophy of Sparrow in the effects of applying ethics to the treatment of robots. Tamvada (2020) connect moral and legal responsibility to accountability in measuring corporate social responsibility.

Negotiating culture in organizational change may be an opportunity for practical philosophical ethics (Brandstedt & Brännmark, 2020). Brandstedt and Brännmark (2020) review the constructivism of Rawl for practical ethics in political philosophy. Paulo (2020) defends the concept of reflective equilibrium from the notion of the unfeasibility of moral institutions. Berman (2021) describes as a contemporary challenge for political science, understanding democratic backsliding and populism.

Negotiating culture in organizational change may also benefit from the review of corporate environments (Kim, Ock, Shin, & Seo, 2018). Kim et al. (2018) propose research in corporate culture for qualitative evaluations of technology. Vamvaka, Stoforos, Palaskas, and Botsaris (2020)apply the theory of planned behavior to analyze

entrepreneurship among demographic groups. Farhadi,
Ismail, and Fooladi (2012) examine the relationship
between information communication technology
consumption and economic growth. Hasan and Koning
(2020) evaluate networks of interaction within
organizations for organizational design interventions.
García-Sánchez, Guerrero-Villegas, and Aguilera-Caracuel
(2019) examine reverse logistics of technological skills in
information technology firms.

References

Abd-Elrhaman, E. S. A., & Ghoneimy, A. G. H. (2018). The effect of conflict management program on quality of patient care. *American Journal of Nursing Science, 7*(5), 192-201.

Addo, A. (2022). Orchestrating a digital platform ecosystem to address societal challenges: A robust action perspective. *Journal of Information Technology,* 02683962221088333. doi:10.1177/02683962221088333

Alexander, N., & Tunkel, N. (2022). International commercial mediation and dispute resolution contracts. *International Commercial Contracts: Law and Practice,* 1-35.

Alexandre Royer, F. F. B., Darlan José Roman, Luccas Santin Padilha. (2020). Transformational leadership for innovation management: A case study of a company winning the Brazil's National Innovation Award. *ELK ASIA PACIFIC JOURNAL OF LEADERSHIP AND INNOVATION MANAGEMENT, 6*(1).

Allcott, H., Gentzkow, M., & Yu, C. (2019). Trends in the diffusion of misinformation on social media. *Research & Politics, 6*(2), 2053168019848554. doi:10.1177/2053168019848554

Alrababa'H, A., Marble, W., Mousa, S., & Siegel, A. A. (2021). Can exposure to celebrities reduce prejudice? The effect of Mohamed Salah on islamophobic behaviors and attitudes. *American Political Science Review, 115*(4), 1111-1128. doi:10.1017/S0003055421000423

Altarriba, J., & Basnight-Brown, D. (2022). The psychology of communication: The interplay between language and culture through time. *Journal of Cross-Cultural*

Psychology, 53(7-8), 860-874.
doi:10.1177/00220221221114046

Angelos, P., Devon, K., Ferreres, A. R., McLeod, R., & Ellison, E. C. (2021). A crucial moment for reflection on the importance of ethical leadership in academic medicine. *Annals of Surgery, 273*(2).

Arrojo, M. J. (2021). Emerging information systems and the design of "iVoz": A case study of enterprise social systems. *Open Journal of Philosophy, 11*, 370-385.

Babalis, T. K., & Lazarakou, E. D. (2021). Employing empathy to teach and assess the learning process in controversial historical issues. *Creative Education, 12*, 1615-1628.

Babri, M., Corvellec, H., & Stål, H. I. (2022). Material affordances in circular products and business model development: for a relational understanding of human and material agency. *Culture and Organization, 28*(1), 79-96.
doi:10.1080/14759551.2021.1986506

Baltaci, A. (2017). Relations between prejudice, cultural intelligence and level of entrepreneurship: A study of school principals. *International Electronic Journal of Elementary Education, 9*(3), 645-666.

Barmeyer, C., Bausch, M., & Moncayo, D. (2019). Cross-cultural management research: Topics, paradigms, and methods—A journal-based longitudinal analysis between 2001 and 2018. *International Journal of Cross Cultural Management, 19*(2), 218-244.
doi:10.1177/1470595819859603

Berman, S. (2021). The causes of populism in the West. *Annual Review of Political Science, 24*(1), 71-88.
doi:10.1146/annurev-polisci-041719-102503

Berry, J. W. (2022). The forgotten field: Contexts for cross-cultural psychology. *Journal of Cross-Cultural Psychology, 53*(7-8), 993-1009.
doi:10.1177/00220221221093810

Blair, G., Littman, R., Nugent, E. R., Wolfe, R., Bukar, M., Crisman, B., . . . Kim, J. (2021). Trusted authorities can change minds and shift norms during conflict.

Proceedings of the National Academy of Sciences, 118(42), e2105570118. doi:10.1073/pnas.2105570118

Boca, G. D., Radulescu, C., Toader, R., & Toader, C. (2015). *A cross cultural model for flexible motivation in management.* Paper presented at the "Dunarea de Jos" University of Galati Fascicle I. Economics and Applied Informatics Years XXI.

Boles, J. R. (2014). The two faces of bribery: International corruption pathways meet conflicting legislative regimes. *Michigan Journal of International Law, 35,* 673-713.

Boon, C., Den Hartog, D. N., & Lepak, D. P. (2019). A systematic review of human resource management systems and their measurement. *Journal of Management, 45*(6), 2498-2537. doi:10.1177/0149206318818718

Bos-de Vos, M., Deken, F., & Kleinsmann, M. (2022). Navigating multiple contexts to integrate system transformation programs. *International Journal of Project Management, 40*(3), 290-311. doi:https://doi.org/10.1016/j.ijproman.2022.03.003

Bouchard, M., Kohler, J. C., Orbinski, J., & Howard, A. (2012). Corruption in the health care sector: A barrier to access of orthopaedic care and medical devices in Uganda. *BMC international health and human rights, 12*(5).

Brandstedt, E., & Brännmark, J. (2020). Rawlsian constructivism: A practical guide to reflective equilibrium. *The Journal of Ethics, 24*(3), 355-373. doi:10.1007/s10892-020-09333-3

Brunelle, E. (2013). Leadership and mobile working: The impact of distance on the superior-subordinate relationship and the moderating effects of leadership style. *International Journal of Business and Social Science, 4*(11).

Bundy, J., Pfarrer, M. D., Short, C. E., & Coombs, W. T. (2016). Crises and crisis management: Integration, interpretation, and research development. *Journal of*

Management, 43(6), 1661-1692.
doi:10.1177/0149206316680030

Ceresia, F., & Mendola, C. (2019). The effects of corruption in entrepreneurial ecosystems on entrepreneurial intentions. *Administrative Sciences, 9*(4). doi:10.3390/admsci9040088

Chan, J. O. (2021). Knowledge management and the pandemic. *International Journal of Business, Humanities and Technology, 11*(1).

Chea, A. (2006). Organizational conflict: Strategy, leadership, resolution framework, and managerial implications. *Journal of Business & Leadership: Research, Practice, and Teaching, 2*(2).

Chiu, C. Y. (2017). Culture matters: A perspective advancing cross-cultural and indigenous research. *Management and Organization Review, 13*(4), 695-701. doi:10.1017/mor.2017.61

Ciuculescu, E.-L. P., & LUCA, F.-A. (2022). How can cultural strategies and place attachment shape city branding? *Cross-Cultural Management Journal, XXIV*(1), 37-44.

Coeckelbergh, M. (2021). Does kindness towards robots lead to virtue? A reply to Sparrow's asymmetry argument. *Ethics and Information Technology*. doi:10.1007/s10676-021-09604-z

Colvin, A. J. S. (2011). An empirical study of employment arbitration: Case outcomes and processes. *Journal of Empirical Legal Studies, 8*(1), 1-23.

Concilio, G., Costa, G., Karimi, M., Vitaller del Olmo, M., & Kehagia, O. (2022). Co-designing with migrants’ easier access to public services: A technological perspective. *Social Sciences, 11*(2). doi:10.3390/socsci11020054

Córdoba-Pachón, J.-R. (2020). Inter-work and ethical vigilance two scenarios for the (post-)pandemic future of systems thinking. *Systems, 8*(36).

Coulmont, M., Berthelot, S., & Talbot, C. (2020). Risk disclosure and firm risk: Evidence from canadian firms. *Risk*

Governance & Control: Financial Markets & Institutions, 10(1), 52-60.

Crandall, K. S., North, M., & Crandall, K. (2020). Digitally transforming the professional school counselor. *Issues in Information Systems, 21*(1), 1-11.

Cronholm, S. (2021). Lifelong learning: Principles for designing university education. *Journal of Information Technology Education: Research, 20,* 35-60.

Dasen, P. R. (2022). Culture and cognitive development. *Journal of Cross-Cultural Psychology, 53*(7-8), 789-816. doi:10.1177/00220221221092409

Dawood, H., Liew, C. Y., & Lau, T. C. (2021). Mobile perceived trust mediation on the intention and adoption of FinTech innovations using mobile technology: A systematic literature review. In: F1000Res.

de la Cuesta-González, M., Froud, J., & Tischer, D. (2020). Coalitions and public action in the reshaping of corporate responsibility: The case of the retail banking industry. *Journal of Business Ethics.* doi:10.1007/s10551-020-04529-x

Della-Piana, G. M., Gardner, M. K., & Mayne, Z. M. (2018). Toward a dialogue following professional standards on education achievement testing. *Journal of Research Practice, 14*(2).

Delpechitre, D. (2013). Importance of cross-cultural empathy in selling – perspective from Asian Indians living in the U.S. *International Journal of Business and Social Science, 4*(11), 15-22.

Dowd, A. C. (2000). Collegiate grading practices and the gender pay gap. *Education Policy Analysis Archives, 8*(10).

Edwards, N., & Saltman, R. B. (2017). Re-thinking barriers to organizational change in public hospitals. *Israel Journal of Health Policy Research, 6*(1), 8. doi:10.1186/s13584-017-0133-8

Erosa, A., Fuster, L., & Restuccia, D. (2016). A quantitative theory of the gender gap in wages. *European Economic*

Review, 85, 165-187.
doi:https://doi.org/10.1016/j.euroecorev.2015.12.014

Erülgen, A., Rjoub, H., & Adalıer, A. (2020). Bank characteristics effect on capital structure: Evidence from PMG and CS-ARDL. Journal of Risk and Financial Management, 13(12). doi:10.3390/jrfm13120310

Essawi, M., & Tilchin, O. (2012). Adaptive collaboration model for organizational change. American Journal of Industrial and Business Management, 2, 145-152.

Farhadi, M., Ismail, R., & Fooladi, M. (2012). Information and communication technology use and economic growth. PLoS One, 7(11), e48903. doi:10.1371/journal.pone.0048903

Fatehi, K., Priestley, J. L., & Taasoobshirazi, G. (2020). The expanded view of individualism and collectivism: One, two, or four dimensions? International Journal of Cross Cultural Management, 20(1), 7-24. doi:10.1177/1470595820913077

Feldman, H. L. (2014). What's right about the medical model in human subjects research regulation. In The Future of Human Subjects Research: The MIT Press.

Fink, L., Shao, J., Lichtenstein, Y., & Haefliger, S. (2020). The ownership of digital infrastructure: Exploring the deployment of software libraries in a digital innovation cluster. Journal of Information Technology, 35(3), 251-269. doi:10.1177/0268396220936705

FitzGerald, C., & Hurst, S. (2017). Implicit bias in healthcare professionals: a systematic review. BMC medical ethics, 18(1), 19-19. doi:10.1186/s12910-017-0179-8

Franco, A. B., & Pound, N. (2022). The foundations of Bolsonaro's support: Exploring the psychological underpinnings of political polarization in Brazil. Journal of Community & Applied Social Psychology, n/a(n/a). doi:https://doi.org/10.1002/casp.2599

Friesenbichler, K. S., & Hoelzl, W. (2022). Firm-growth and Functional Strategic Domains: Exploratory evidence for differences between frontier and catching-up economies. *Journal of Economics and Business, 119*, 106033. doi:https://doi.org/10.1016/j.jeconbus.2021.106033

García-Sánchez, E., Guerrero-Villegas, J., & Aguilera-Caracuel, J. (2019). How do technological skills improve reverse logistics? The moderating role of top management support in information technology use and innovativeness. *Sustainability, 11*(1). doi:10.3390/su11010058

Gelfand, M. J., Aycan, Z., Erez, M., & Leung, K. (2017). Cross-cultural industrial organizational psychology and organizational behavior: A hundred-year journey. *Journal of Applied Psychology, 102*(3), 514–529.

George, B., Walker, R. M., & Monster, J. (2019). Does strategic planning improve organizational performance? A meta-analysis. *Public Administration Review, 79*(6), 810-819. doi:https://doi.org/10.1111/puar.13104

Gerhart, B. (2009). How much does national culture constrain organizational culture? *Management and Organization Review, 5*(2), 241-259. doi:10.1111/j.1740-8784.2008.00117.x

Glover, J., & Guerrier, Y. (2010). Women in professional IT jobs in the UK: Old wine in new bottles? *2010, 5*(1), 10. doi:10.4067/s0718-27242010000100007

Gordon, B. G. (2020). Vulnerability in research: Basic ethical concepts and general approach to review. *Ochsner Journal, 20*(1), 34. doi:10.31486/toj.19.0079

Green, D. P., & Seher, R. L. (2003). What role does prejudice play in ethnic conflict? *Annual Review of Political Science, 6*(1), 509-531. doi:10.1146/annurev.polisci.6.121901.085642

Gürerk, Ö., Irlenbusch, B., & Rockenbach, B. (2018). Endogenously emerging gender pay gap in an experimental teamwork setting. *Games, 9*(4), 98.

Hall, C. B., Brazil, K., Wakefield, D., Lerer, T., & Tennen, H. (2010). Organizational culture, job satisfaction, and clinician turnover in primary care. *Journal of Primary*

Care & Community Health, 1(1), 29-36.
doi:10.1177/2150131909360990

Hamdani, J. (2021). Factors Affecting the Entrepreneurial Dynamics. *Journal of Global economics, 9*(2).

Harikkala-Laihinen, R. (2022). Hooked on a feeling? An interpretive study of organizational identity (dis)continuity during strategic change programmes†. *International Journal of Project Management, 40*(3), 262-277.
doi:https://doi.org/10.1016/j.ijproman.2022.03.004

Harris, A., Pattillo, M., & Sykes, B. L. (2022). Studying the system of monetary sanctions. *RSF: The Russell Sage Foundation Journal of the Social Sciences, 8*(2), 1.
doi:10.7758/RSF.2022.8.2.01

Hasan, S., & Koning, R. (2020). Designing social networks: Joint tasks and the formation and endurance of network ties. *Journal of Organization Design, 9*(1), 4.
doi:10.1186/s41469-020-0067-4

Haslinda, A. (2009). Evolving terms of human resource management and development *The Journal of International Social Research, 2*(9), 180-186.

Herrington, M., & Coduras, A. (2019). The national entrepreneurship framework conditions in sub-Saharan Africa: A comparative study of GEM data/National Expert Surveys for South Africa, Angola, Mozambique and Madagascar. *Journal of Global Entrepreneurship Research, 9*(1), 60. doi:10.1186/s40497-019-0183-1

Hoshiro, H. (2020). Do diplomatic visits promote official development aid? Evidence from Japan. *Political Science, 72*(3), 207-227.
doi:10.1080/00323187.2021.1948344

Huang, L. (2010). Cross-cultural communication in business negotiations. *International Journal of Economics and Finance, 2*(2).

Huang, X., de Vliert, E. V., & der Vegt, G. V. (2005). Breaking the silence culture: Stimulation of participation and employee opinion withholding cross-nationally.

Management and Organization Review, 1(3), 459-482. doi:10.1111/j.1740-8784.2005.00023.x

Iivari, N., Sharma, S., & Ventä-Olkkonen, L. (2020). Digital transformation of everyday life – How COVID-19 pandemic transformed the basic education of the young generation and why information management research should care? *International Journal of Information Management*, 102183. doi:https://doi.org/10.1016/j.ijinfomgt.2020.102183

Inegbedion, H., Sunday, E., Asaleye, A., Lawal, A., & Adebanji, A. (2020). Managing diversity for organizational efficiency. *SAGE Open, 10*(1), 2158244019900173. doi:10.1177/2158244019900173

Israel, M. J., & Amer, A. (2021). Ethical implications of digital infrastructures for pluralistic perspectives. *Ethics and Information Technology*. doi:10.1007/s10676-021-09582-2

Jaramillo, P., Rascon, M., Adams, C., & Jauregui, E. (2020). Fundamental principles, processes, and roles of environmental qualification test strategy for complex engineered systems. *Journal of Information Technology & Software Engineering, 10*(265).

Ji, Q. (2022). Effects of BLM on students' reading proficiency: An empirical study among vocational college students based on POA. *Open Access Library Journal, 9*.

Karp Gershon, S. a., Ruipérez-Valiente, J. A., & Alexandron, G. (2021). Defining and measuring completion and assessment biases with respect to English language and development status: not all MOOCs are equal. *International Journal of Educational Technology in Higher Education, 18*(1), 41. doi:10.1186/s41239-021-00275-w

Kästner, B., Behre, S., Lutz, N., Bürger, F., Luntz, S., Hinderhofer, K., . . . Ries, M. (2015). Clinical research in vulnerable populations: Variability and focus of institutional review boards' responses. *PLoS One, 10*(8), e0135997. doi:10.1371/journal.pone.0135997

Keet, C. M., & Grütter, R. (2021). Toward a systematic conflict resolution framework for ontologies. *Journal of Biomedical Semantics, 12*(1), 15. doi:10.1186/s13326-021-00246-0

Kim, E., Ock, Y. S., Shin, S.-J., & Seo, W. (2018). An approach to generating reference information for technology evaluation. *Sustainability, 10*(9). doi:10.3390/su10093200

Kimseng, T., Javed, A., Jeenanunta, C., & Kohda, Y. (2020). Applications of fuzzy logic to reconfigure human resource management practices for promoting product innovation in formal and non-formal R and D firms. *Journal of Open Innovation: Technology, Market, and Complexity, 6*(2). doi:10.3390/joitmc6020038

Korenkiewicz, D., & Maennig, W. (2022). Women on a corporate board of directors and consumer satisfaction. *Journal of the Knowledge Economy.* doi:10.1007/s13132-022-01012-y

Kuehnel, K., & Au-Yong-Oliveira, M. (2022). The Development of an Information Technology Architecture for Automated, Agile and Versatile Companies with Ecological and Ethical Guidelines. *Informatics, 9*(2). doi:10.3390/informatics9020037

Kwet, M. (2020). Fixing social media: Toward a democratic digital commons. *Markets, Globalization & Development Review, 5*(1).

Laakso, M., & Polonioli, A. (2018). Open access in ethics research: An analysis of open access availability and author self-archiving behaviour in light of journal copyright restrictions. *Scientometrics, 116*(1), 291-317. doi:10.1007/s11192-018-2751-5

Lafaire, A. P., Kuismin, A., Moisander, J., & Grünbaum, L. (2022). Interspace for empathy: Engaging with work-related uncertainty through artistic intervention in management education. *Culture and Organization, 28*(3-4), 227-244. doi:10.1080/14759551.2022.2029442

Leal Filho, W., Wall, T., Barbir, J., Alverio, G. N., Dinis, M. A. P., & Ramirez, J. (2022). Relevance of international partnerships in the implementation of the UN Sustainable Development Goals. *Nature Communications, 13*(1), 613. doi:10.1038/s41467-022-28230-x

Lewin, A. Y. (2014). Emerging economies open unlimited opportunities for advancing management and organization scholarship. *Management and Organization Review, 10*(1), 1-5. doi:10.1111/more.12048

Ličen, M., & Slapničar, S. (2022). Can process accountability mitigate myopic biases? An experimental analysis. *Journal of Management Control.* doi:10.1007/s00187-021-00330-7

Liu, X. (2016). A literature review on the definition of corruption and factors affecting the risk of corruption. *Open Journal of Social Sciences, 4*, 171-177.

Lv, L., Liu, Z., & Xu, Y. (2019). Technological progress, globalization and low-inflation: Evidence from the United States. *PLoS One, 14*(4), e0215366. doi:10.1371/journal.pone.0215366

Ma, R. W. Y., & Cheng, E. C. K. (2020). Psychological contracts, work behaviour and turnover intention in the Hong Kong telecommunications industry. *Universal Journal of Management, 8*(4), 119-130.

Mabovula Nonceba, N. (2011). The erosion of African communal values: A reappraisal of the African Ubuntu philosophy. *Inkanyiso, 3*(1), 38-47. doi:10.10520/EJC112680

Madva, A. (2016). A plea for anti-anti-individualism: How oversimple psychology misleads social policy. *Ergo, 3*(27), 701-728.

Manstead, A. S. R. (2018). The psychology of social class: How socioeconomic status impacts thought, feelings, and behaviour. *The British journal of social psychology, 57*(2), 267-291. doi:10.1111/bjso.12251

Maseko, T. S. B. (2017). Strong vs. Weak organizational culture: Assessing the impact on employee motivation. *Arabian Journal of Business and Management Review, 7*, 287.

Maury, B. (2022). Strategic CSR and firm performance: The role of prospector and growth strategies. *Journal of Economics and Business, 118*, 106031. doi:https://doi.org/10.1016/j.jeconbus.2021.106031

Mayowa, A. O. (2020). A Basis, Data Oriented and Frame For Actionable Decision Making In Management. *Journal of Organizational Culture, Communications and Conflict, 24*(3).

McKenzie, J. (2022). The economics of movies (revisited): A survey of recent literature. *Journal of Economic Surveys, n/a*(n/a). doi:https://doi.org/10.1111/joes.12498

Mhaskar, R., B Bercu, B., & Djulbegovic, B. (2013). At what level of collective equipoise does a randomized clinical trial become ethical for the members of institutional review board/ethical committees? *Acta informatica medica : AIM : journal of the Society for Medical Informatics of Bosnia & Herzegovina : casopis Drustva za medicinsku informatiku BiH, 21*(3), 156-159. doi:10.5455/aim.2013.21.156-159

Mirbabaie, M., Bunker, D., Stieglitz, S., Marx, J., & Ehnis, C. (2020). Social media in times of crisis: Learning from Hurricane Harvey for the coronavirus disease 2019 pandemic response. *Journal of Information Technology, 35*(3), 195-213. doi:10.1177/0268396220929258

Mittal, S. (2016). Role of mobile phone-enabled climate information services in gender-inclusive agriculture. *Gender, Technology and Development, 20*(2), 200-217. doi:10.1177/0971852416639772

Momanyi, D. K., & Juma, D. (2016). The influence of conflict management strategies on employee satisfaction: A case study of KCB Bank Kenya Limited, head office. *International Academic Journal of Human Resource and Business Administration (IAJHRBA), 2*(2), 130-144.

Morehouse, J. (2020). Stakeholder-formed organizations and crisis communication: Analyzing discourse of renewal with a non-offending organization. *JOURNAL OF INTERNATIONAL CRISIS AND RISK COMMUNICATION RESEARCH, 3*(2), 243–274.

Mousseau, D. Y. (2021). Globalization and the prevention of ethnic wars at the local level: A cross-country analysis. *Negotiation and Conflict Management Research, 14*(3), 187-206.

Mudave, E. (2016). Information Literacy (IL) learning experiences: A literature review. *Inkanyiso, 8*(1), 57-68. doi:10.10520/EJC192235

Mühlhoff, R. (2021). Predictive privacy: Towards an applied ethics of data analytics. *Ethics and Information Technology.* doi:10.1007/s10676-021-09606-x

Naranjo-Cantabrana, M. G., Ayala-Bobadilla, N. P., & Castro-Borunda, Z. I. (2014). Organizational diagnosis with gender mainstreaming in the Instituto Tecnológico de los Mochis, period 2013. *Ra Ximhai, 10*(5), 255-264.

Negoita, B., Rahrovani, Y., Lapointe, L., & Pinsonneault, A. (2021). Distributed IT championing: A process theory. *Journal of Information Technology,* 02683962211019406. doi:10.1177/02683962211019406

Nerlinger, A. L., Shah, A. N., Beck, A. F., Beers, L. S., Wong, S. L., Chamberlain, L. J., & Keller, D. (2018). The advocacy portfolio: A standardized tool for documenting physician advocacy. *Academic Medicine, 93*(6).

Nyholm, S. (2018). The ethics of crashes with self-driving cars A roadmap, II. *Philosophy Compass, 13.*

Oguejiofor, J. O. (2012). African and Greek philosophy: A pristine dialogue in search of contemporary relevance: Special theme articles. *Phronimon, 13*(2), 55-72. doi:10.10520/EJC128690

Omar Bali, A. (2018). Communication tools to fight bureaucratic corruption in Iraqi Kurdistan: A case study. *SAGE Open,*

8(4), 2158244018811185. doi:10.1177/2158244018811185

Opie, T., & Roberts, L. M. (2017). Do black lives really matter in the workplace? Restorative justice as a means to reclaim humanity. *Equality, Diversity and Inclusion, 36*(8).

Orlitzky, M., Louche, C., Gond, J.-P., & Chapple, W. (2015). Unpacking the drivers of corporate social performance: A multilevel, multistakeholder, and multimethod analysis. *Journal of Business Ethics, 144*(1), 21-40. doi:10.1007/s10551-015-2822-y

Oye, N. D. (2013). Reducing corruption in African developing countries: The relevance of e-governance. *Greener Journal of Social Sciences, 3*(1), 6-13.

Page, S. A., & Nyeboer, J. (2017). Improving the process of research ethics review. *Research Integrity and Peer Review, 2*(1), 14. doi:10.1186/s41073-017-0038-7

Pager, D., & Shepherd, H. (2008). The sociology of discrimination: Racial discrimination in employment, housing, credit, and consumer markets. *Annual Review of Sociology, 34*, 181-209. doi:10.1146/annurev.soc.33.040406.131740

Paolella, L., & Durand, R. (2016). Category spanning, evaluation, and performance: Revised theory and test on the corporate law market. *Academy of Management Journal, 59*(1), 330-351. doi:10.5465/amj.2013.0651

Park, S., Nam, C. M., Park, S., Noh, Y. H., Ahn, C. R., Yu, W. S., . . . Rha, S. Y. (2018). 'Screening audit' as a quality assurance tool in good clinical practice compliant research environments. *BMC medical ethics, 19*(1), 30. doi:10.1186/s12910-018-0269-2

Patton, C. M. (2018). Changes: A conflict management model for organizational redesign efforts. *Journal of Conflict Management, 6*(1), 26-40.

Paulo, N. (2020). The unreliable intuitions objection against reflective equilibrium. *The Journal of Ethics, 24*(3), 333-353. doi:10.1007/s10892-020-09322-6

Pedrosa, A. L., Bitencourt, L., Fróes, A. C. F., Cazumbá, M. L. B., Campos, R. G. B., de Brito, S. B. C. S., & Simões E Silva, A. C. (2020). Emotional, behavioral, and psychological impact of the COVID-19 pandemic. *Frontiers in Psychology, 11*, 566212-566212. doi:10.3389/fpsyg.2020.566212

Popoola, T., & Karadas, G. (2022). How impactful are grit, i-deals, and the glass ceiling on subjective career success? *Sustainability, 14*(3). doi:10.3390/su14031136

Prieto-Díeza, F., Postigoa, Á., Cuestaa, M., & Muñiz, J. (2022). Work engagement: Organizational attribute or personality trait? *Journal of Work and Organizational Psychology, 38*(2), 85-92.

Puiu, S., & Ogarca, R. F. (2015). Ethics management in higher education system of Romania. *Procedia Economics and Finance, 23*, 599-603. doi:https://doi.org/10.1016/S2212-5671(15)00564-X

Quffa, W. A. (2016). A review of the history of gender equality in the United States of America. *Social Sciences and Education Research Review, 3*(2), 143-149.

Quirico, O. (2021). Disentangling conflicts of laws in EU and member states' investment agreements. *Journal of Dispute Resolution*(2).

Ralefala, D., Ali, J., & Kass, N. (2018). A case study of researchers' knowledge and opinions about the ethical review process for research in Botswana. *Research Ethics, 14*(1), 1 –14.

Randall, P. M., Lartey, F. M., & Tate, T. D. (2020). Enterprise social media (ESM) use and employee belongingness in US corporations. *Journal of Human Resource Management, 8*(3), 115-124.

Resnik, D. B., & Elliott, K. C. (2016). The ethical challenges of socially responsible science. *Accountability in research, 23*(1), 31-46. doi:10.1080/08989621.2014.1002608

Robison, J. (2022). Valuing politics: Explaining citizen's normative conceptions of citizenship. *Political Behavior*. doi:10.1007/s11109-022-09773-7

Rohilla, J. (2017). Role of information technology in human resources management. *International Journal of Advance Research, Ideas and Innovations in Technology, 3*(2), 566-569.

Romani, L., Mahadevan, J., & Primecz, H. (2018). Critical cross-cultural management: Outline and emerging contributions. *International Studies of Management & Organization, 48*(4), 403-418. doi:10.1080/00208825.2018.1504473

Roy, D. (2021). Formulation of governance and democracy index (GDI) and governance, democracy, and emancipation index (GDEI): A cross-country empirical study (1998 – 2017). *Open Political Science, 4*(1), 15-26. doi:doi:10.1515/openps-2021-0002

Sawa, R. (2020). A prospect theory Nash bargaining solution and its stochastic stability. *Journal of Economic Behavior & Organization.* doi:https://doi.org/10.1016/j.jebo.2020.11.009

Shah, I. A., Amjed, S., & Jaboob, S. (2020). The moderating role of entrepreneurship education in shaping entrepreneurial intentions. *Journal of Economic Structures, 9*(1), 19. doi:10.1186/s40008-020-00195-4

Shah, S. T. H., Shah, S. M. A., & El-Gohary, H. (2022). Nurturing innovative work behaviour through workplace learning among knowledge workers of small and medium businesses. *Journal of the Knowledge Economy.* doi:10.1007/s13132-022-01019-5

Siebert, E. C., & Herbst, U. (2021). New perspectives on issue analysis—one-sided preferences as a strategic source in multi-issue negotiations. *Negotiation Journal, 37*(4), 485-518. doi:https://doi.org/10.1111/nejo.12379

Smith, P. B., & Bond, M. H. (2022). Four decades of challenges by culture to mainstream psychology: Finding ways forward. *Journal of Cross-Cultural Psychology, 53*(7-8), 729-751. doi:10.1177/00220221221084041

Somerville, K., Cinite, I., & Largacha-Martínez, C. (2021). Organizational change skills: An empirical cross-national study. *Open Journal of Business and Management, 9*, 894-911.

Sousa, M. J., Marôco, A. L., Gonçalves, S. P., & Machado, A. D. (2022). Digital learning is an educational format towards sustainable education. *Sustainability, 14*(3). doi:10.3390/su14031140

Subramanyam, M., & Dasaraju, H. (2014). Corporate governance and disclosure practices in listed information technology (IT) companies in India. *Open Journal of Accounting, 3*, 89-106.

Suelzer, E. M., Deal, J., Hanus, K., Ruggeri, B. E., & Witkowski, E. (2021). Challenges in identifying the retracted status of an article. *JAMA Network Open, 4*(6), e2115648-e2115648. doi:10.1001/jamanetworkopen.2021.15648

Sugianto, A., & Pontjoharyo, W. (2020). Lean accounting in transforming the organizational culture in PT. A. *IJRDO - Journal of Business management, 6*(9).

Tagaki, M. (2017). Action research on drafting municipal policies for people with disabilities in Japan. *SAGE Open, 7*(3), 2158244017723050. doi:10.1177/2158244017723050

Tamvada, M. (2020). Corporate social responsibility and accountability: a new theoretical foundation for regulating CSR. *International Journal of Corporate Social Responsibility, 5*(1), 2. doi:10.1186/s40991-019-0045-8

Taylor, W. C., Suminski, R. R., Das, B. M., Paxton, R. J., & Craig, D. W. (2018). Organizational culture and implications for workplace interventions to reduce sitting time among office-based workers: A systematic review. *Frontiers in public health, 6*, 263-263. doi:10.3389/fpubh.2018.00263

Tsai, Y. (2011). Relationship between organizational culture, leadership behavior and job satisfaction. *BMC Health Services Research, 11*(98).

Urquhart, E. (2019). Technological mediation in the future of experiential tourism. *Journal of Tourism Futures, 5*(2), 120-126. doi:10.1108/JTF-04-2019-0033

Vähä-Savo, V., Luomanen, J., & Alasuutari, P. (2022). Between rationalism and romanticism: metaphors in managing conflicting institutional logics in science and technology parks. *Culture and Organization, 28*(1), 46-63. doi:10.1080/14759551.2021.1969650

Vamvaka, V., Stoforos, C., Palaskas, T., & Botsaris, C. (2020). Attitude toward entrepreneurship, perceived behavioral control, and entrepreneurial intention: dimensionality, structural relationships, and gender differences. *Journal of Innovation and Entrepreneurship, 9*(1), 5. doi:10.1186/s13731-020-0112-0

van Gestel, N., Oomens, S., & Buwalda, E. (2019). From quasi-markets to public–private networks: Employers' engagement in public employment services. *Social Policy & Administration, 53*(3), 434-448. doi:https://doi.org/10.1111/spol.12469

Wang, N., & Wu, G. (2020). A systematic approach to effective conflict management for program. *SAGE Open, 10*(1), 2158244019899055. doi:10.1177/2158244019899055

Whitehorn, A. (2020). Conflict resolution in healthcare settings: Staff conflicts. *The Joanna Briggs Institute EBP Database, JBI.*

Woodhouse, E. F., Belardinelli, P., & Bertelli, A. M. (2022). Hybrid governance and the attribution of political responsibility: Experimental evidence from the United States. *Journal of Public Administration Research and Theory, 32*(1), 150-165. doi:10.1093/jopart/muab014

World Economic Forum. (2016). The industry gender gap women and work in the fourth industrial revolution.

Zhang, D., & Xie, Y. (2022). Customer environmental concerns and profit margin: Evidence from manufacturing firms. *Journal of Economics and Business, 120*, 106057. doi:https://doi.org/10.1016/j.jeconbus.2022.106057

Zhang, N. (2022). How does CSR of food company affect customer loyalty in the context of COVID-19: a moderated mediation model. *International Journal of*

Corporate Social Responsibility, 7(1), 1.
doi:10.1186/s40991-021-00068-4

Zheng, Q., & Chun, R. (2017). Corporate recidivism in emerging economies. *Business Ethics: A European Review, 26*(1), 63-79. doi:10.1111/beer.12132

Made in the USA
Coppell, TX
03 September 2022